JONAH AND THE WHALE

Ella K. Lindvall

© 1994 by
THE MOODY BIBLE INSTITUTE
OF CHICAGO

This story has been extracted from
Read-Aloud Bible Stories, vol. 4

Illustrated by
H. Kent Puckett

Printed in Mexico

MOODY PRESS

Jonah was not happy.
Jonah said,
"I don't want to do
what God says.
I will run away."

*Step, step,
step, step,*
Jonah hurried
down the road.
Jonah got on a boat.
Away went the boat
on the blue water.
God saw Jonah go.
God knew
what Jonah needed.

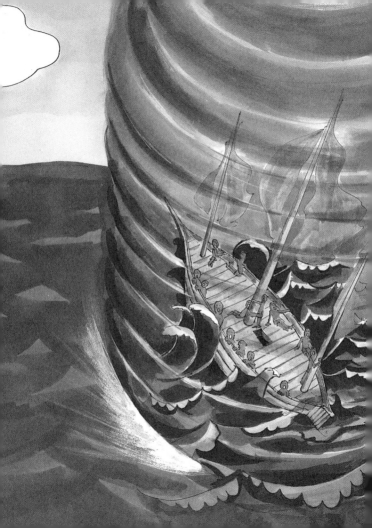

So God sent
a big wind
to help him.
Who-o-o.
God's wind blew
on the water.
Who-o-o.
God's wind blew
at the boat.
Who-o-o.
The water went
SPLASH!
Everybody got wet.

The men worked hard
to make the boat go.
But it wouldn't.
The men were afraid.
They said,

"SOMEBODY has done something wrong. That is why this big wind is trying to upset our boat. WHO IS IT?"

Then Jonah said,
"I did it.
I was trying
to run away
from God.
Just throw me
into the water.
Then the wind
will stop."

The men worked hard
to make the boat go.
But it wouldn't.
So they did
what Jonah said.
They picked him up.
They threw him
into the water.
SPLASH!
And then—

the wind did stop going
who-o-o, who-o-o.
The water did stop going
splash, splash.
The big storm went away
—all of it.

Now God knew
what Jonah needed.
God sent a big fish
to help him.
The big fish
opened its mouth—
WIDE.
It gobbled up Jonah
in ONE BITE!
Oh, my.
Did *that* help Jonah?
Yes, it did.

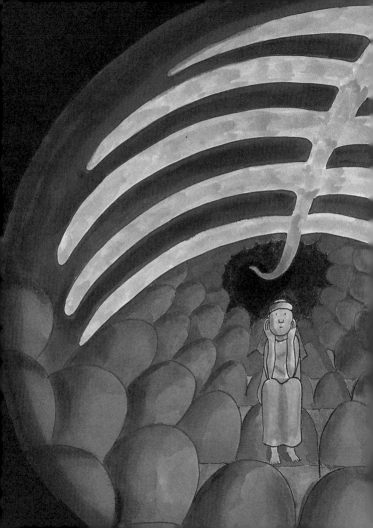

The next thing
Jonah knew,
there he sat
safe inside
the big fish.
It was dark.
It was wet.
Jonah didn't like it
in there.
But Jonah was safe.

Down, down, down
went the fish.
Down, down, down
went Jonah.
Then Jonah
talked to God.
"Help me, Lord,
and I will do
what You told me
to do."

Now God knew
what Jonah needed.
God told the fish,
"TAKE JONAH BACK
TO THE LAND."
The fish did
what God said.
After a while
it opened its mouth—
WIDE.

And the next thing
Jonah knew,
there he sat
on the nice dry sand.

Jonah stood up.
He looked around.
He saw the blue sky.
He saw the sunshine.
He saw the trees.
He thanked God.
And then—

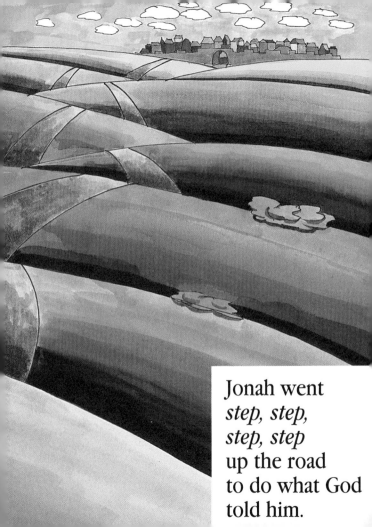

Jonah went
*step, step,
step, step*
up the road
to do what God
told him.

What did you learn?

God knew what Jonah needed.
He sent the big wind to help.
God knew what Jonah needed.
He sent the big fish to help.
God knows what you need.
He wants to help you too.

About the Author

Ella K. Lindvall (A.B., Taylor University; Wheaton College; Northern Illinois University) is a mother and former elementary school teacher. She is the author of *The Bible Illustrated for Little Children*, and *Read-Aloud Bible Stories*, volumes I, II, III, and IV.